The Flower Oracle

by

Atalanta

With a foreword by Jules Leman

ingeborg creations
u.k.

Copyright © Atalanta 2010

Published by
ingeborg creations

The author, Atalanta, has asserted her right under the Copyright Design and Patent Act 1988 (and under any comparable provision of any comparable law in any jurisdiction whatsoever) to be identified as author of this work.

All rights reserved. No part of this publication may be reproduced by any mechanical, photographic, or electronic process, or in the form of a phonographic recording; nor may it be stored in a retrieval system, transmitted, or otherwise be copied for public or private use – other than for "fair use" as brief quotations embodied in articles and reviews - without prior written permission of the publisher. The intent of the author is only to offer information of a general nature to help you in your quest for emotional and spiritual well-being. In the event you use any of the information in this book for yourself, which is your constitutional right, the author and the publisher assume no responsibility for your actions.

ISBN-13: 978-0-9571101-0-6
ISBN-10: 0957110103

ingeborg creations
West Sussex. RH17 6ER.
info@ingeborgcreations.com

Contents

Contents

***

Foreword by Jules Leman…vi

***

Preface…viii

***

The guide to using 'The Flower Oracle'…10

***

Anticipate Miracles…12
Apple-pie Order…14
Blessings…16
Bounty…18
Celebration…20
Commitment…22
Cornucopia…24
Dependency…26
Duplicity…28
Embarkation…30
Fairy Enchantment…32
Fragility…34
Good Fortune…36
Have Faith…38
Hurrah…40
Indecision…42
Intemperance…44
Junk old karma…46
Liberation…48
Longevity…50
Magnetism…52
New Opportunities…54

Nurture Yourself...56
Oodles of Plenty...58
Out with the Old, In with the New...60
Patience...62
Peregrination...64
Perseverance...66
Protection...68
Quicksilver...70
Resplendent...72
See the Funny Side...74
Self-Esteem...76
Slow and Steady...78
Spirituality...80
Take Care...82
The Law of Attraction...84
Think Positive...86
Transformation...88
True Love...90
Unique...92
Verification...94
Wonderment...96
Your Choice...98

***

Affirmations...100

***

Small Flower Oracle Cut-Outs ...101

***

Large Flower Oracle Cut-Outs...103

Foreword

I met Atalanta over 15 years ago during my time living in England. As a Clairvoyant and Psychic Medium I frequently visited the S.A.G.B. in London from my then home in Hertfordshire and it was no coincidence that our paths crossed. We spent many special times together connecting to spirit and sharing inspiration. During one visit I met Atalanta's Mother, who now lives a busy life in the Spirit World. Like her daughter, not only was she incredibly intuitive but also a talented gardener, as I was to find out when I was invited to a function at her home.

I was immediately overwhelmed by the sense of serenity as I walked into the garden. In fact the whole area surrounding the home is a sanctuary of healing, a magical place; and my little secret to you is that the flowers within this book are taken from there.

At the time of publishing Mother Nature is outdoing herself and daily we hear of natural disasters, which provoke pain and questions, yet, in balance, and somewhat taken for granted by many of us on a daily basis she also offers wonderment and answers. Atalanta has captured this essence with her inspiring oracle.

In our overcomplicated, overbusy, overworked world, we find ourselves looking for inspiration that can tell us what we need to know clearly, simply and quickly. Whenever Atalanta undertakes a project it is perfectly timed and spiritually blessed, and if you follow her wisdom, you will receive healing and guidance from this book.

I now live in New Zealand and work as a Spiritual Medium and Clairvoyant, delivering workshops and private readings to clients internationally and would wholeheartedly offer this book to clients inspired by the flower world.

… and from the world of Spirit, Mother nods
her beautiful head.

Blessings,

Jules

August 2011
www.julesleman.com

Preface

Modern Spiritualism is a philosophy based on an understanding of spirit. It is a way of thinking that is non-restrictive, nonconformist and encourages you to take more notice of your intuition or gut reactions. Modern Spiritualism is there to encourage and support you, with love, to do your best and find balance in your life.

Although I was brought up as a Spiritualist, believing that seeing and hearing spirits was quite normal, in those days tarot cards, Ouija boards and such-like were quite often frowned upon. The thinking was that they were evil or sinister and could in someway bring misfortune.

When I was eventually old enough to have a reading done for me by a medium who used tarot cards, I was quite relieved to discover that I didn't suffer any harm as a result!

Later on I did buy myself some oracle cards, but I found that they were very restricted to traditional pictures of Angels and deities I'd never heard of or other 'magical' images, and also that quite often they didn't answer my questions.

I decided that it was time for a present day, modern oracle. I found all that imagery rather old-fashioned and fussy, and so did friends of mine who held different religious beliefs, but who still wanted a tool to tap into, to use their spirituality to divine answers to their concerns. I wanted an oracle that would give insight, answer questions and have complementary illustrations that weren't off-putting. Seeing that if I needed a link in to help me give someone a reading, I used flowers, it seemed quite straightforward to me what I needed to do.

Thus 'The Flower Oracle' was born, and I do hope you enjoy this, and that it answers what you need to know.

Atalanta
6th September 2010

I Dedicate 'The Flower Oracle'

To

My Wonderful Son Alfred,

My Good Friend Selvam

&

My Beautiful Mother

With

Grateful Thanks & Love

x x x x x x

The guide to using 'The Flower Oracle'

As easily as tarot cards and tea leaves can be used to connect with the spirits and initiate a reading, flowers (when used in a reading) provide a truly natural way of linking into spirit. 'The Flower Oracle' uses spiritual interpretations to answer the questions that you have.

This book contains two sets of Flower Oracle Cut-Outs; one large and one small. You first need to choose which size you prefer, and then go ahead and cut along the dotted lines. If you do not want to cut them out of the book, you can go to www.thefloweroracle.com to download extra Cut-Outs. Once cut, it is suggested that you fold them firmly over in half, twice each.

You need to prepare your Flower Oracle Cut-Outs before using them for the first time. Choose a quiet time when you can sit down and won't be disturbed. Place all the Cut-Outs into your cupped hands and say either out loud or in your head: -

"Almighty Universe,
please guide me to use 'The Flower Oracle'
with love, courage and integrity.
Thank you for giving me great protection and
showing me what I need to see.
Thank you for these blessings.
Amen."

You can tailor what has been written here with your own beliefs. For instance, where it says 'Universe' you can substitute the name of whichever God you believe in.

Now with all the Cut-Outs in your cupped hands, you are ready to ask the question which is uppermost in your mind. Shake them whilst repeating what you want to know, again either out loud or in your head. Then drop them onto a flat surface in front of you, asking for the Cut-Out that answers your question to be made clear to you.

See which one you are drawn to. If you are not drawn to any particular one, gather them all back into your hands and ask again to be shown a clear answer. Pay attention to the one that has dropped to a space of its own. You will be able to see which one is most prominent and can then consult the appropriate page in the book for its meaning.

'The Flower Oracle' works best with specific questions. It is always better to approach using it when you are as relaxed as possible and in a quiet space. If you are very worked up about something, your aura will be clouded and you will have a block around you. So it is important, no matter how concerned you are, that you manage to calm yourself down, in order to be open to receiving advice.

Equally do not use "The Flower Oracle' to answer other people's questions when you are preoccupied with your own affairs. Ego needs to be left behind at all costs.

You may like to keep the Cut-Outs in a bag or a bowl, and take one out at random when asking your question. You may also find that you are drawn to more than one Cut-Out. Perhaps in asking your question, one falls prominently in front of you with another one wrapped around it. Refer to the interpretations for both of the Cut-Outs and see how they work together to answer your concern.

There is no wrong or right way to use 'The Flower Oracle' just so long as your intention is genuine. The more you use them, invariably you will find your own preferred method, but do remember that the calmer you are when you ask your question, the better.

When 'The Flower Oracle' is used correctly in conjunction with your own gut-feelings, intuition or spirituality (however you wish to term it) you will feel comfortable with your decisions, which will in turn give you inner contentment and purpose.

Anticipate Miracles

Have faith in yourself and the Universe
will hear you and respond

Anticipate Miracles

Although your path has not been smooth, know that you can anticipate miracles. Your path in the future, once you have weathered the storms, has only good ahead for you. If you have been wishing for miracles your prayers are being answered.

Things have been tough for you for so long now that you have shut yourself off, in some way, from other people and kept yourself private.

Now is the time to venture forth, as you only have this one life. You need to live your life, and go forward with confidence.

There is so much love ahead of you. The seeds that you have sown can grow if only you allow them to. Have faith in yourself and the Universe will hear you and respond.

The more you ask the Universe for help and anticipate the glorious outcome, the sooner your situation will improve.

You have a lot of love and security ahead of you. Now is the time to claim it. Realise that, in your life, you have never been given anything which you couldn't deal with. If you think about it properly, you will admit that you have always got through any trials or tribulations that you've been faced with.

Drawing this Cut-Out shows that now is the time for you to accept your present situation. For all the untidiness and complications that you may have around you, it is right for you to gather your strength and stand up proudly.

Anticipate the miracles and solutions that you have asked for. Know that the Universe will respond with love for your Highest Good. Be especially open to opportunities that come along which you weren't expecting.

Always remember to be thankful for your path being smoothed, and to give thanks for each good thing that happens to you, no matter how trivial it seems, as that will multiply the frequency of them occurring.

Apple-pie Order

Time to claim your own power
and take control of your life

Apple-pie Order

Your life is so busy and hurried that you are barely giving yourself enough time to think - let alone look after yourself properly. What is needed here is some 'Apple-pie Order'.

What this means is that you need to prioritize all the elements of your life in a more structured way. You are over stretching yourself. It seems that you are being called on and, to a certain extent, put upon in all the different areas of your life. Enough! It is time for you to take control of your own life.

Running around and being so busy is exhausting you. If you do not take care, your neglect of your own well-being will make you ill.

It is no bad thing to preserve yourself and stop being at everyone's beck and call. You have been kept so busy of late that you have lost sight of your own spiritual welfare.

You need to pay more attention to your own life. There are some magical opportunities around you, but in being so concerned with other matters, you have turned your back on progressing in your own life.

You have a lot of natural spiritual ability, which you are not using to your best advantage. You are aware of your capabilities but do not seem to have fully accepted them.

Time to stop and appreciate yourself. Picking this Cut-Out means that the concerns which you have, can be resolved by spreading yourself less thinly and concentrating on areas that are of greater concern to you. Apply yourself fully to what is unsettling you, and by drawing on your spirituality you can meditate and ask for clear guidance and direction. Ask for your solution to be made clear to you and then listen for signs and act on them.

You are a good soul. Claim your own power and take control of your life. You have inner wisdom and now is your time to use it.

Blessings

A significant blessing is there for you

Be sure to accept it

Blessings

A significant blessing is there for you. It is so close. Either you are aware of it now - or you soon will be.

If you have a matter that is concerning you there are indications that someone is coming to your assistance. There is a genuine offer of help for you, so please do not pass it up.

Every day it is possible to count your blessings. From little things such as enjoying a nice view, getting an unexpected smile from a stranger or even just finding a parking space; to bigger things such as solving a major problem or dilemma.

Try taking a notebook with you and write down each blessing as it happens. This will concentrate your mind on the positive aspects of your life which will, in turn, benefit you greatly. The more you notice and express gratitude for your blessings, the more they will increase. Each day is a new beginning that allows you to start afresh.

If your concerns are about love, apply 'new' to your situation and know that it is good. Find new ways of sharing love and pepping things up. Expect and accept new love into your life. The more love you give out, without conditions, the more love you will receive. Love is all around you if you open your eyes and acknowledge it.

If you have concerns about your work situation, be objective and do your best to bring harmony into your working environment and apply yourself. If it is a new venture that you seek - do it, as it is well aspected, and if you seek help you will be given it - so forge ahead!

In health and other concerns, seek out the relevant experts that you can learn from - they are probably closer to home than you realise. By taking small steps in the right direction, you will be helped and you need not fear.

Move forward with positivity, as the Universe will provide the help that you need.

Bounty

Creative abundance is bubbling up
in your life

Bounty

You are on a new pathway in your life. There is an abundance of some type bubbling up for you right now.

This new part of your life you may not have given much thought to, but once the seed of it has got into your mind, you will find that it just runs away with you.

One thing will lead to another and you will find yourself, as a result, embarking on areas that you may not have even considered before.

There is an abundance of thought here. Bounty of this type can also signify a new blessing - either a new home - a new job or business - or even a new baby.

With this change comes a wealth of future promise, which will also have the effect of introducing new people, places or things into your life.

The Heavens are pleased with this adjustment and you have nothing to fear. The situation that you are concerned about needs a fresh way of looking at it, in order to enable the change which needs to come in.

There is nothing to be frightened about as your situation is surrounded by the love of the Universe. This means that no matter how troubled you may feel - it is temporary. You are in a time when you can 'start that book' 'write that movie' 'begin that business' or even 'bake that cake'!

This is all about constructive new activities or undertakings in your life all stemming from your own creativity.

You have no time to lose. Do not procrastinate as that suggests a fear of failure. Banish any doubts and let yourself explore and grow into new ideas. The Universe is willing you to get on with things. Carry a notebook and write down anything that helps to inspire and carry you forward.

This is an exciting time for you, as what you create now will open up avenues to a multitude of new experiences.

Celebration

You have the freedom to step forward on
your life path with added enthusiasm

Celebration

Wow! The Heavens have opened up to you and now is cause for great celebration!

Time to bask in the light of success. Whatever your concerns are, be assured that your ultimate outcome is a reason for festivities.

Particularly well-favoured are relationships. Time to rejoice for the love in your life. Recognize and be thankful for all the romance that surrounds you. Even if not apparent, take time to understand what you can be grateful for. Smile at all those you meet and count how life returns your intentions.

This is very much concerned with adult matters. In work concerns you will get support when you follow your heart.

In financial matters, you are supported and inspired when you follow a philosophy or example that you can aspire to.

In matters of the heart, you can achieve your dreams with a like-minded soul, as long as you give each other a certain amount of freedom.

All is abundant and well-placed. Your goals are all achievable and you can thank your Guardian Angel for answering your inner wishes.

By celebrating you also allow yourself to relax and enjoy. Happiness is there for you in profusion and you are invited to kick back and let your hair down - you deserve it!

There is a lot ahead of you, which is being kept under wraps. By acknowledging and having fun, your path will clear and you will be able to see which direction you should take. You will always shift onwards and upwards as long as you are thankful and appreciative of everything that is in your life.

You are worthy of all that you have and all that you are about to receive. Justification could not be clearer.

You have the freedom to step forward on your life path with added enthusiasm. Time to celebrate!

Commitment

This is your time to come forward and
make positive decisions

Commitment

Drawing this Cut-Out denotes that there is a commitment issue in your life. Whatever question you have it is now time to either dedicate yourself fully to the situation or decide to quit. Whichever side your feelings fall on, in this matter, what is needed from you is a proper commitment to your decision.

In matters of the heart, it may be that you have been putting up with things almost out of habit. If you distance yourself and look at your situation, it will become plain to you whether the relationship is worth keeping. If so, it needs you to make positive steps towards bringing harmony and romance back into your relationship, where it appears lacking.

Or it may be that you have lost your own self-worth by being treated like a doormat and taken for granted. If this is the case you have to get out and start expressing your own individuality - perhaps by taking a course or a new job.

Whatever you do, you need to get fully behind your decision. Being totally engaged in another area of your life will then allow you to look at your love life in a more balanced way, and help you to make decisions.

In work or money matters, look carefully at the situation as you do not seem to be pushing yourself forward. You are sitting back and allowing the situation to develop around you, instead of taking control and applying practical measures.

If money is short, undertake to see where you can spend less and what positive steps you can take to alleviate and help your situation.

This Cut-Out says that the solutions are there for you if you pledge to do something positive about things. This is not a situation where someone else can solve it for you. This is your time in life to come forward and be fully committed. Know that if you are unsure, put your request out and trust the Universe to make the path clear to you that you need to follow.

Cornucopia

The abundance of the Universe is there
waiting for you to claim it

Cornucopia

Be thankful and know that you are truly worthy, as picking this Cut-Out indicates a profusion of abundance is available for you. The Universe is awaiting your instructions, as there is a well of plenty for you to receive.

If you have been praying or asking for help about something, then you must re-evaluate the way in which you have been addressing your needs. It is all very well vocalizing or thinking about the desperate situation that you may be in, constantly airing your fears, troubles and doubts.

However, the Universe has no interest in indulging these negativities, as that will only give you more of the same. What they need to hear from you are your hopes and dreams. They need to hear what your real intentions are in your life, so that your Angels may empower you and manifest your aspirations. It is as simple as that.

If work is your issue, then with application your dreams can be realized and success achieved. If there are any problems that you are experiencing, apply a lightness of touch to maximize your potential.

Love is very well starred. You will be able to luxuriate in love and enjoy great passion. You are either with your true soul mate, or they will be coming into your life.

In money matters, follow your dreams with complete faith and conviction, and you will reap the benefits. There is no room for doubt or irrational fear, as this will block you from receiving.

Health requires you to love and cosset yourself, which will enable the best to be attained for you within your life path.

The Heavens want you to see the lightness in your situation. Great happiness is there for you, and also well-deserved time and opportunities for you to relax, enjoy and laugh. It is all there waiting for you. The key is for you to feel truly worthy, grateful and accepting.

Dependency

Time to ditch that obsession
to set yourself free

Dependency

You are such a beautiful person, but you are involved in something that isn't helping you.

There is a dependency of some type in your life. Whatever your concerns are, you need to apply the rationale that there is an aspect of it that you keep repeating in your life, and that this is hindering you.

Are you addicted to alcohol? Drugs? Overeating? A person who doesn't return your feelings? A job that is wearing you down? Are you being lazy and letting life pass you by? Be truthful and ask yourself what is it that you are hooked on? What is causing your unhappiness?

You need to get tough with yourself. It is so easy to get stuck in a way of thinking or living that isn't beneficial to you.

If you think, "better the devil you know than the devil you don't" then now is the time to ditch that negative mantra and embrace all the good that life has to offer you.

You most definitely can move forward in life and achieve what is right for you. Your dependency is what is holding you back. It seems to have been going on for a long time and you need to let go. Put an end to it and that will set you free.

There are many organizations that help with various addictions that you can turn to. If your problem is of a different type then seek out someone such as an acquaintance, family member, colleague or friend that you can talk to, as it will help you to confide in someone that you can trust. You will also find it easier to break your habit with the aid of someone else giving you much needed encouragement and supporting you.

There are new spheres for you to get involved in. Once you do away with whatever it is that you are obsessed with, your life will open out. You will find greater happiness and your life is well starred for equal shares of serenity and personal success.

Duplicity

Be sensible and take your time
as there is a duality about your situation

Duplicity

Things are not as they seem. There is a duality about your situation. Whatever your question, you need to be aware that things are not as straightforward as you think they are.

If your question is about money, then no matter how hard things seem for you, there is someone there to help you if you let them. But make sure that everything is totally above board and proper, otherwise you could get deceived.

Or if it is a finance deal that you are signing, make sure that it is on the level, and that you understand and agree to all the terms and conditions. Take your time to read it properly, and do not sign in haste.

If your question is about love or work, apply the same thoughts. Be aware of your situation and the help that is available. Make sure that whatever deals or relationships you get into, you comprehend and are wise to everything around you.

Choosing this Cut-Out alerts you that there is a duplicity in your situation. Know that you need to be aware that whomever is by your side, take off your rosy glasses and see them as they really are, and not as you would like them to be. There may be someone else that they are thinking of, and if this is a problem to you - let them go so that you may move forward and find the right person to be with.

The Universe is asking you to be sensible and take your time. Although deception of any type is never pleasant to cope with, this is no bad thing as you are being warned in advance. The Universe is protecting you and giving you the tools to help you to deal with how things really stand.

Therefore, realise that your Angels are watching over and safeguarding you. Be strong and sharp-witted in your dealings and, ultimately, you will benefit from this life lesson that you have learnt.

Embarkation

A significant change of direction brings
blessings and fulfillment

Embarkation

There is a change of direction on the cards for you. An embarkation on a new pathway.

This is a fresh beginning for you, which is significant. You will be leaving things behind and indications are that this is an important move for you, which will also demand your full attention. There is nothing to fear, however, as you are fully equipped to deal with your new situation. Be it moving home or changing your career, this is likened to a breath of fresh air for you, as it is very well aspected. You can only grow and benefit from this transformation of your life. Although it may necessitate that you leave loved ones behind, ultimately you have their support, as this is right for you.

If you have been wishing for something for a long time, this is the change that you need to allow to happen, in order for you to realise your dreams. Don't think it is an instant fix, because you are just at the start and need time to pass in order to expand.

If love is your concern this indicates the beginning of a new relationship. Or if you are already involved, then perhaps there is a new way of looking at your relationship that would be more beneficial, or even a new baby - although signs are that this is a singular journey and something that you need to do for yourself.

Citrine is a very good crystal to wear close to your skin at this time, as it is warming, energizing and highly creative. This dynamic stone also helps with manifestation and attracts wealth and prosperity, success and all good things.

There is a clear path for you to follow in the question that concerns you, which will ultimately fulfill all your needs. Give thanks for your blessings, as this is a brand new phase of your life that you are commencing upon, which will allow you to leave old karmic situations behind and start afresh.

Fairy Enchantment

Mystical magic is being weaved
around your situation

Fairy Enchantment

Never underestimate the power of fairy enchantment. You may not be aware of them, but they are weaving mystical magic around your situation right now.

These little trooping fairies are here to inspire you with love and communication. They want to lift you out of the situation that troubles you and get you to see the bigger picture. They want you to speed up your vibration, as you seem to be at a low ebb. Make sure that you are looking after your body - eating properly, having enough vitamins and drinking plenty of water.

Realise that although your concern may feel big, it is nothing compared to what you can achieve with determination and love. These spirits of nature want to connect you with the earth. They want you to feel more grounded and secure, as they are itching to send you invigorating and uplifting inspiration.

They want you to see what creative avenues you can follow. They want to encourage you to spread your wings and seek more out of your life. You are very capable, but seem to have forgotten what joy being creative can bring.

Magic has long been associated with the nature spirits because magic is simply the art of manifestation. If you were to ask a fairy, they would most certainly tell you that humankind learnt it all from them - after all, they were the ones that manifested all of nature…?!

Therefore, capture the fairies' confidence and positivity and channel your thoughts to the highest possibilities. Do not think small - think big, and you can achieve more than you dream of.

Surround yourself with positive thoughts and loving feelings. Reach for the sky and expect the very best that miracles can accomplish.

Fragility

Follow your head not your heart and
deal with what you need to do

Fragility

Knowledge is within your reach about the concerns that you have, but it seems that you are, to an extent, a little blinkered or hesitant to actually face what needs to be done. You feel stuck and at a loss as to what to do now. Time has passed you by and there is a sadness around your situation. Your fellow birds have, metaphorically, flown the nest, and yet you are still there waiting to be fed.

There is an air of fragility around you, which means that now is not a time for well-meaning friends or advisors to be browbeating you into action. What is needed is patience and kindness applied to your concerns.

If it is a concern of the heart that you have, you need to consider your own happiness. Is it repairable? Will that make you truly content? Life has to be figured out and what suited you before may not necessarily suit you now. Inner contentment is needed.

With financial concerns your heart is in the right place, but you are allowing the situation to run away with you, and are not shouldering your real responsibilities. You need to face up to things and take out a proper loan or solid solution, instead of wishing your problems away. Any other matters that you may be anxious about, apply the reasoning that you need to be less airy-fairy about events. Think with your head and not your heart, however well-founded you may feel that to be. Decisive action needs to be faced and taken, in order to achieve what you really want.

Don't let life pass you by. It is a good thing to have dreams and aspirations, and the Heavens want to hear what you intend to achieve in your life. Your requests for help are being answered, but it is imperative that you listen to your inner voice and instead of getting lost in your dreams, do something concrete towards a solution. You will ultimately win through.

Good Fortune

Your prayers are being answered
Expect the unexpected

Good Fortune

Great abundance is coming your way. Expect the unexpected. The Universe is giving you what you have long been wishing for. A stroke of luck that you were not anticipating is on its way to you right now.

You may have felt that your prayers were falling on deaf ears. What you cannot see is how your Spirit Guides have been working tirelessly to get things in place for you.

Although you have been trying hard at the matter that concerns you, it's almost as if you have tied yourself up in knots. The more you have wished and tried to get what you want, the more tangled up you have become.

Your prayers are being answered. Don't get disheartened, as you need to be ready to accept your windfall. All will be made clear given time.

There is an element of doubt creeping through and you have to lose any uncertainty in order to be clear to receive.

In all aspects of your life where you feel dubious of a positive outcome, you need to re-focus your thoughts on the optimistic or beneficial end result.

Don't be afraid for believing in the best. This is your life and what you focus your thoughts on has a habit of manifesting tenfold. So be grateful and thank the Universe for answering your prayers.

A good affirmation to help you is, "I accept and delight in all the good and abundance that is flowing into my life. I am very grateful." Repeat this frequently to aid the good that is there for you. Every thought you have is a chance to make the life you want to lead. Keep confident and consciously turn your negative thoughts into positive ones.

Your prayers are being answered - which must truly be a cause for celebration. Remember this and be happy and grateful to receive!

Have Faith

There are abundant times ahead
Trust that it will all work out to your Highest Good

Have Faith

You are being doubtful and therefore putting up barriers to being helped. Your Guardian Angel needs you to ask for his help before he can intervene.

Have faith. Accept Heaven's help and your path will become clear.

Let go of your fears and doubts. The longer you hold onto thoughts of what you dislike and don't like in your life, the longer you will continue to keep what you do want away.

Have courage to let go of your fears and worries, and have faith that when you ask for Spirits' help, they will assist you and give you guidance.

If you have a specific wish, ask the Spirits to help you with the proviso 'to my Highest Good'. This allows events to happen for you as they should, and doesn't block out your future unfolding as it is meant to.

Be sure that, in picking this Cut-Out, if you take its advice your future ahead will be joyous and abundant. You have a good future ahead and your wishes will come to fruition in a plentiful way if you stop stressing and allow Heaven to help you. Ask for their help and it will be given.

For a long time you have been stubborn in being almost obsessively protective of your position. This stance may actually be reinforcing your lack of money/love/health in focussing on your own scarcity in these areas. This Cut-Out urges you to release your fears and have faith in the Universe.

This problem seems to have gone on for a while and will carry on for longer until you have faith and ask for the Universe to intervene and give you assistance. You need to then let go and allow them to help you. Pay attention to your intuition and open up. Be positive. There are abundant times ahead.

Above all have faith and trust that all will work out to your Highest Good.

Hurrah

Let the future unfold as it should
You are one in a million!

Hurrah

You are one in a million! Did you know that? In whatever area you are concerned about, you are going to end up winning.

Sure, life can sometimes feel monotonous. Day after day seeming the same. Nothing ever quite moving, making you feel stuck. Your prayers not seemingly being answered...

Stop right there! You are on the brink of success. You are being Divinely guided to be in the correct place at the perfect time. What you need to do is to stay strong and have faith in your positive outcome.

The Universe has expected and unexpected ways of answering our appeals for help. In order to help your resolution to come into fruition, it is necessary for you to release any set ideas you may have for how the Universe is going to answer your needs, as this is blocking you.

Instead, you need to open yourself up to all opportunities - but please don't waste your precious time imagining all possible scenarios. This is a misuse of your valuable time.

You seem rather resistant, almost as if you need a push to go forward. Freeing yourself and allowing the Universe to do its own thing, may make you feel useless because you will think that you are not doing anything productive towards helping yourself. But the very fact that you have enough faith to let go and trust, will release you to greater things.

Drawing this Cut-Out means that the Heavens are willing you to succeed. Accept all opportunities that come your way.

Say 'yes' to unexpected invitations or opportunities to get out and mix with new faces. Make the effort and it will open your life up and pay dividends.

There is so much satisfaction, enjoyment and success there for you. Don't waste any more time. Allow your future to unfold the way it is meant to.

Indecision

Move forward with confidence as you are greatly
protected and have nothing to fear

Indecision

Although you don't see it at the moment, if you sit down and think objectively about your life you will see that there has never been a time (no matter how dreadful or seemingly impossible) when you haven't come through in the right way for you. The situation now, that you find yourself concerned over, is no different.

Although you haven't had a smooth run of things during recent times, if you compare your life to others less fortunate than yourself, you will see how blessed you really are.

In your present situation you have great protection from the Universe, and it is clear that you are being steered in a particular direction. However, you seem apprehensive and even a little disdainful about the path you are being asked to take. You need to stop being so proud and self-important, and loosen up, because if you do you will find that you will gain a lot more than you would ever have thought possible. You really can afford to let your hair down and enjoy yourself.

You are so protective of yourself that you run the danger of blocking out possible new friendships and alliances. You are a beautiful person and by shielding yourself so carefully, you are not allowing all the abundance to come in that is waiting for you. Deep down inside you are a real softie, which makes you even more special because that means you have a big heart - compassionate and loving.

Have courage and let yourself open up to the world around you. Go with the flow and take steps to make a go of the options that you have. What you do now will lead onto better things. Ahead of you is the realization of your dearest wishes, but on a far higher level than you have been asking for. Thank your lucky stars for all your dreams coming true and move forward with confidence, because you certainly have great protection and nothing to fear.

Intemperance

Time to take stock and use your willpower to heal
the situation that you are concerned about

Intemperance

You have been over-doing it in some way and are not listening to what loved ones, or those who are in authority are saying to you. This is a very hard time for you to pick this Cut-Out as it is telling you to stop and listen, and chances are that you just don't want to. You are actively turning away from those who want you to see what you are doing that is impeding your life right now.

You have the whole world at your fingertips but you need to stop excessing. Whether it is obsessing over someone or, equally, running around after somebody, it is now time for you to stop. You are never too old to change. Even though what is troubling you is deep-seated, it is never too late to change direction.

You have almost grown into the situation that you find yourself in. Perhaps from slavish devotion or from old outmoded ways of behaving and believing, you seem to have let time pass you by and have neglected yourself.

If you have put on weight - you can lose it if you put your mind to it. If you are stuck in a financially vicious trap - you can make a concerted effort to revise your situation. If you have not thought yourself worthy and have stuck with the same job/partner/way of life - then now is the time to take stock of your situation, be brave and change what you are doing.

The answer to your problem is deep-rooted and you will have a large part of you that is resistant to change. But please remember that each moment is new and you are in control, ultimately, for what you do. You are the master of your own fate and your mind is the most powerful force. You are able to change your way of thinking and do something positive about your position, right now, if you want to.

This is the time to believe in yourself and your own abilities by exercising your willpower.

Junk old karma

Release yourself from past negativity so that
you are free to follow your destiny

Junk old karma

Things are looking good for you, yet you seem to be unsure. Your situation is telling you to go forward and accept, and yet you aren't. You have issues in your past, which are actually holding you back right now. Even with the best will in the world, you cannot move forward until you have made peace with your past and dealt with the old karmic issues that you have allowed to linger.

If you continue to let old associations and criticisms stay in your psyche it will not help you in your future life, and may even cause future problems to arise, which you otherwise would not have. You are actually destined for a very bright future. However you have had someone or something that has clouded your life in a very forceful way and whether you are admitting to it or not, this affects the way you view things.

Although you are capable of forging ahead if you so want to in your present circumstances, if you continue to ignore your past inhibitions you will not be free. This will hamper you progressing fully and you will, more than likely, keep repeating the same mistakes over and over again.

You do not have to carry the burden of former conflicts unless you insist on doing so. You can call upon Archangel Camael* in meditation, and ask him to cancel your concluded karma so that you are free to follow your life path. As long as you are respectful and have pure intent, then by asking you may find that you will be set free from your completed karma.

An affirmation to help you is, "I release all past negative patterns, fear and doubt. I am strong, clear and open. I receive abundance, love, light and knowledge. Thank you Life."

All your dreams are possible for you to achieve, you just have to be resolute about ridding yourself of the old negative beliefs or patterns that continue to limit you. Your future is in your hands.

*pronounced Car-my-ell

Liberation

Live in the now and set yourself
free to receive

Liberation

Outwardly things look bright and promising for you, so what is holding you back? To find the answers to your concerns you need to look at yourself first.

Throughout your life you have had to deal with more than your fair share of problems - difficulties interspersed amongst the good times. It seems that although your future potential is abundant, you are more than a little being held back by feelings of regret and grievance.

The opportunity is there, right now, for you to rid yourself of past struggles and move forward. Although the question is - do you really want to? Are you aware of these old ways of thinking which trigger negative feelings? Are you just too comfortable with holding onto the past?

Time to let go and free yourself. Monitor your thoughts and every time you find yourself thinking or saying things that refer to past events, mentally interrupt yourself. Focus your thoughts on the moment you are in.

When you find yourself thinking about old issues, repeat this affirmation, "The past is finished and gone. I control my life. I choose to think clearly and positively. I live in the now."

There are also indications that you have been holding yourself back from communicating with others. There are people, places and things that are so close to coming into your life. Once you have thrown off your past thinking shackles and committed to living each moment fully present in the now 'doors will be opened', 'new love will come', 'you will meet people who you are more in tune with' or, in other words, life will just simply open up for you.

Be grateful for the present life that you are living and know that by letting go of all old negativity, you are releasing old insecurities and liberating yourself to lead the life that you want to.

Longevity

There is spirituality around your situation
You can achieve miracles

Longevity

This Cut-Out denotes spirituality around your situation. You are in the right place at the perfect time, which means that at this point in your life you are meant to be dealing with this concern. There is longevity in the direction that you want to go in. It is almost like the beginning of something, even though you have already commenced.

Education and learning are well starred and will be very beneficial to you. Embarking on long-term plans, however small they may seem to you at this moment, will expand your horizons to greater things over time.

If you feel stuck and cannot see what to do, use meditation (or if that is not your thing - just sit quietly and seek direction). Ask for what you need to do next to be made clear to you. As long as you ask, that will allow your Spirit Guides to help you and they will steer you in the right direction.

If you have specific concerns look at your situation with a view to where, in an ideal world, you would like to be in ten years' time. Then, no matter how gigantic and far away your goals seem, if you begin to break down into practical steps a strategy that you can follow, it will allow you to focus on how to achieve your aspirations in a more measured and attainable way. Treat it rather like writing a book; you have to work out where you want your story to go and then how to make it happen. Do the same for your aspirations. The Universe wants you to be active in what you do even if, ultimately, you may change direction. You need to be out there doing something constructive, right now, in order to attain your dreams.

This is therefore not a time for impatience, but a time for practical application. Do not be scared of moving forward and exploring new vistas. This is your life and your time to be looking at the bigger picture. It is up to you to strike out for what you really want. Have courage. Achieve those miracles.

Magnetism

Sheer enchantment surrounds your
situation right now

Magnetism

This is your time! You are ready to receive all the good that you have been wishing for. However, there is an element about you that seems to be counterproductive to what you really want. It is almost as if you say one thing - but do the other.

Time to get real and stop shrinking away and accepting less. You are on the point of great success in all areas of your life, but what you seem to be doing is undermining your attainment of what you really want.

Let go of all fear. You are blocking your situation by not acknowledging how wonderful you are! Don't put yourself down - that is such a waste of your precious energy.

Whatever it is that you are asking about, know that now is the time to push yourself forward and receive. The time is right to 'be with that person', 'start that new business' or 'make that move'. Know that you are fully equipped to achieve your dreams. Stop hesitating and making excuses. Get on with the matter at hand.

The Universe is supporting you and urging you to move forward with your life. Don't hide away. You have got so much good in front of you, but you do have to make an effort in order to draw the abundance that is there for you into your life.

Don't be disheartened by past events. Things or people were not right for you at that time. But every cloud has a silver lining, and events have shown that despite everything, you are well protected by the Universe.

There is an aspect of sheer enchantment around your situation right now. Come out of your shell and accept the influence of the Heavens!

You have a lot to give and a lot to receive. Remember that what you give out comes back to you multiplied. Therefore believe in yourself and accept Heaven's help without delay.

New Opportunities

Stay honest in your intentions and
let life guide you

New Opportunities

You are not stuck. There are a multitude of possibilities and opportunities up ahead for you. Stay focused and know that you are safe. Ask for help from your Guardian Angel to hear their advice and see the choices up ahead for you.

It seems that you have been asking for the right things to happen to you for a long time. Know that this is possible and that the Heavens have heard you and are acknowledging your requests. However, everything needs to happen at the right time and there is an element that suggests that you will have to wait a little while longer. Deep down your intention is clear and as long as you have integrity about that which you ask, you cannot fail.

If it is love you are after be aware and recognize that 'Actions speak louder than words'.

For work issues, as long as you are sincere in your what you do, the truth will out.

For health issues, divulge your worries to the appropriate person/health professional, and you will find your strength and be able to progress forward in the way you were meant to.

This Cut-Out shows that, for whatever concerns you may encounter, inside you have a heart of gold. This means that, whatever your concerns, they may be easily overcome as you have a multitude of possibilities and opportunities ahead of you which can ultimately lead you to where you wish to be.

You have to be firm in your resolve and accepting in your fate. Always be sure that what you wish for is to your Highest Good. Stay honest in your intentions and you will have a clearer route in life to follow.

Life, ultimately, gives you what you wish for. So make sure that your wishes are without preconditions and you will not be disappointed. Accept your new opportunities as they come and let life guide you. You are safe.

Nurture Yourself

Now is the time to be gentle with yourself and
listen to your body

Nurture Yourself

Now is the time to be gentle with yourself. Nurture your body and be sure that the truth will out in the situation that concerns you.

Therefore listen to your body. No problem is worth sacrificing your own health and well-being over. If you do not look after yourself properly, then you are neglecting the most important force in your life – You! You need to gather your strength and be kind to yourself, if you are going to live your life to your full potential. If you ask for guidance, you will be given it. Your Sister of Mercy is waiting to guide you and ensure that your way will be smoothed.

Choosing this Cut-Out indicates that you are especially being told to look after yourself. It is necessary for your spiritual growth and development, let alone your life. No matter what your situation, be true to yourself and listen to your body. You have concentrated on your concerns and worries so much that you have neglected yourself, and your body needs to be nourished and nurtured. Look after yourself and hand over your concerns to your Sister of Mercy. If you let go and trust that you are safe and well protected, then you will be.

Now is a good time to indulge yourself in soothing pastimes. Set some time aside just for you. Switch the answerphone on and run a deep bath filled with calming bath salts. Light candles and burn incense. Calm and centre yourself. Directly talk to your Sister of Mercy. Tell her what troubles you and then give it over to her. Ask her to surround you with the 'Christ White Light of Protection'. Trust and try not to force the issues. If you truly let go and have asked for help and guidance, then it will be given.

For assurance in your situation affirm, "I am safe and secure. Well protected and guided. I look after myself and my life is smooth and abundant."

Oodles of Plenty

You are a very fortunate individual
Claim your abundance

Oodles of Plenty

Sometimes, in life, you need to concentrate on working hard, and sometimes you need to sit back and accept and receive all the good results of what you have been working hard towards. This Cut-Out indicates that you need to be doing both, but with greater clarification.

Whatever your concerns are, you need to approach them in a sensible, pragmatic way. You are on the tip of receiving great rewards, but you need to make it clearer to the Universe what you expect your outcome to be. The Universe has oodles of abundance to give to you, but you need to focus your requests more patently. Strangely, some of your past desires are still available to you, waiting in the ether so to speak.

If your concerns are about work, stick with it and make sure that you have pursued each available option, as you will soon be experiencing the fruition of all your hard work. This is a good time for growth and expansion. You are also well advised to explore areas that you can expand into, as you will benefit greatly from this. Keep working and doing things in the way that you normally do, as you are on the right path and do not have to change anything apart, that is, from being clearer about your intentions and choices.

If your concerns are love-related, then children figure quite strongly. There are good indications for your situation. However, the first relationship you should have is with your *self*. You must learn to honour, cherish and love your *self* first. Please make sure you never do anything in your relationship out of a sense of obligation. Do whatever you do out of the awareness of the magnificent opportunity your relationship allows you to choose and to be really, who you truly are.

You are a very fortunate individual. The key is to be clear about your choices and then go and get them. All the abundance of the Universe is waiting for you.

Out with the Old, In with the New

It is time for you to de-clutter your life

Out with the Old, In with the New

This Cut-Out carries promise of abundant new pastures, once you have de-cluttered your life - be it possessions, people or beliefs.

It is time for you to take stock and see what you do not need or what holds you back in life - then get rid of it.

Now is the time to be brave and throw out any old beliefs or ways of thinking that may have worked for you before, but are not serving you now. Look at the way you think and turn each negative thought into a positive one.

It is safe for you to allow change into your life. It takes courage and determination, but there are things in your life that seem to be holding you back and blocking you from progressing any further. Listen to your intuition and if you are unsure, ask the Universe for firm indications to tell you what you need to eliminate from your life.

There is no need to fear because when something goes out of your life, the space it leaves behind allows new things to come in. As long as your intentions are genuine there is no need for any anxiety.

If your concerns are financial, see what you can do to eliminate waste and unnecessary spending, and then see what you can do to help yourself.

If it is love that is concerning you, are you with the right partner? If you feel that you are, what can you do to make your relationship more loving? Or if you don't believe in your relationship, now is the time to move on.

If you are searching for that special someone, examine ways in which you could get yourself out meeting people, so that you may be in the perfect place at the right time.

Quit resisting. De-clutter and let go. Empower yourself. Get rid of what is holding you back in life, to leave space for what you really want to come in.

Patience

Stay calm – this is not something that
can be solved quickly

Patience

Have patience. The situation that you have been worrying about will sort itself out. What is needed is time.

Sometimes you have to let things go that you love. You cannot blame others for your situation because, ultimately, you do things of your own free will. What has brought you to where you are now is the sum of your own actions.

Equally you cannot live someone else's life for them. You may advise and help but, in the end, they will do what they want to do.

If you love them you will let them go and allow them to plough their own furrow. That doesn't stop you from being in the background, if they need your love and understanding.

Picking this Cut-Out tells you that you are well protected. Understand that the Universe loves you. Your concerns will not overwhelm you.

The Universe advises that you stay calm and realise that this cannot be solved quickly. You need patience as this will take time to unravel. One of the truest sayings is that 'Time is a great healer', and you are being told that your situation requires time.

Use your time to calm yourself down. Find the positive for each situation. Do not dwell on the negative. Persevere for the right outcome. Now is not the time to be forceful, as that will not get you anywhere. Maintain your dignity. If you feel tempted to act quickly try to restrain yourself. The more composed and cool-headed you can keep yourself, the better.

Be grateful for what you *do* have in your life and take the time to look after yourself in body, mind and spirit. Be gentle on yourself. Know that the Universe is looking after you and has heard your prayers.

Don't act in haste. Let the Universe guide you and answer your prayers to your Highest Good.

Peregrination

You are on the move and this movement
of travel brings welcome changes in for you

Peregrination

You're on the move. There is a lot of travel ahead for you. This Cut-Out indicates travel so strongly that it may have a wider implication in your life. In the very simplest explanation of picking this Cut-Out, a holiday is imminent for you. A much needed break away from home. A chance to recharge your batteries and kick back your heels. You deserve this time and it will help to bring balance back into your life.

If your concerns are work related then either you are travelling with your job or need to look at other options where you can get more involved and spread your wings. Different areas that you can move into will widen your knowledge and capabilities.

If someone is troubling you then don't hold onto the heartache. Get yourself out of their vicinity and give yourself time to consider your options. If any movement of you, your ideas, attitude or mindset can be made, then it will allow you to experience better composure and mental equilibrium

With the movement of travel, comes shifts in ideas and perceptions. It also indicates that letting go of fixed ideas which you have, opens you up to better stability. There is a promise of spiritual fulfillment if you so wish. Taking time out to meditate and connect with your Spirit Guides is of great benefit to you. You are also invited to consider practicing astral travel, as that will allow your Soul to be liberated.

The Universe is shining light and love on you right now. Accept that travelling, either physically or mentally, will bring you happiness and satisfaction, which comes as a result of fully developing your abilities or character. You will broaden your horizons and be able to consider options that you didn't know were there. If your situation has felt fragmented, you now have the opportunity to consolidate your life. This will ultimately lead to self-confidence and balance.

Perseverance

You may feel stuck now but don't quit
- you will get there in the end

Perseverance

This is a long-term Cut-Out denoting that you have been stuck in a situation for a protracted amount of time. Whatever your concern may be, what is certain is that you have come to a standstill, almost like treading water.

Feeling stuck in this way can make you doubt your own abilities and can cause you to feel very low and worn out. Please know that there is light at the end of the tunnel. You are not stuck forever.

If you have lost someone close to you, then you need to know that Spirit would want you to persevere and fulfill your life potential. Have faith that the love surrounding you from Spirit will help you through this.

In financial matters, you need to rid yourself of the things that are draining your resources. Also it is important for you to be true to your instincts, through discovering ways to build your income up. What you take time over now has every chance of growing in due course. You have talents and abilities that have been hidden for far too long. Now is a good time to start expressing yourself creatively.

Your steadfastness can overcome the circumstances that you are in. Applying determination and dedication will reap rewards as long as you realise that, as with anything that is worth having, this will take time.

If you feel you are in a 'Yes' or 'No' situation, apply the logic that out of bad comes good, and then visualize a positive outcome in order to help it manifest.

If you have been hurt in some way - whether bodily or emotionally - healing takes time, but know that you will indeed repair, if that is what you truly wish for.

Have the courage to follow your dreams. You will reap rewards if you persevere. Time is a great healer. Don't quit just yet. You are nearly there!

Protection

Let the Angels take control and guide you

You are safe

Protection

You have weathered the hard times and are stronger as a result. By asking to be safe and praying for protection, the Heavens have heard you and your prayers are being answered. Let the Angels take control and guide you. Be still and listen for inner guidance.

There are triumphant times ahead. The sum of all your actions have brought you to where you are now.

In matters of the heart, you can allow yourself to be the child in the relationship. Your love of life is endearing and captivating. If you wish for love but are not presently in a relationship, then you soon will be. Your love is liable to take you in many directions - so try not to get too giddy!

In money and work-related matters you will find opportunities that will surprise and delight you. Prepare to be stretched in more than one direction. Because you are Divinely protected there is nothing which comes your way that you are not able to deal with. Have courage and faith that the Universe is protecting you and that you are more than qualified to move forward.

You have inner strength which is borne out of all the trials and tribulations that you have overcome. Do not feel nervous. Know that you can achieve your goals ahead.

Watch that your thoughts are positive. Practice daily affirmations into a mirror to reinforce constructive thought patterns. Focus on what you really want and vocalize it in the present tense. For example, "I deserve my abundant life and I am very grateful that I manifest money easily."

Although you are not completely out of your troubles, they are lessening and will soon be behind you.

Watch that you don't put up barriers to allowing new things or people into your life. Know that you are safe to start to enjoy what you have and relax.

Quicksilver

Time to learn to choose your experiences
and delight in what you can achieve

Quicksilver

You have been trying very hard to achieve what you want in the matter that concerns you, but things haven't been working out as you envisaged they would. Your situation has moved so fast that it seems out of your reach. This has caused you distress.

This is not the first time that this has happened to you. You need to ask yourself why this pattern is repeating itself? Do you secretly accept and like to experience your life in this way? Is this what you, in reality, expected from the start?

You can do, think and say out loud what you want all the time, but if you do not absolutely believe that it is true - it won't happen. Life is a creation and not a discovery. You always get what you create and you are always creating. It is also true to say that you attract what you fear.

For example, before every miracle Jesus would thank God in advance for it happening. It never crossed his mind not to be grateful, because it never occurred to him, that what he said wouldn't happen. The notion never entered his mind.

If you apply this clarity to what you think, say and do, you will be a force to be reckoned with. If there is something that you want to experience in your life, take a different way of approaching things, and instead of wanting it - *choose* it. You will be amazed at what you can achieve if you truly and fully choose. Don't be half-hearted, because in order to fully receive remember that you get back what you put out.

You have a good heart and a sunny disposition, which can carry you through to make the right choices in life. Trust that what you feel in your heart is correct and choose to believe in your own self-judgement. Try not to take on too many tasks and commitments at the same time. Concentrate on one thing at a time, in order to completely focus your thoughts and actions. Choose your life experience. It will be glorious!

Resplendent

Always follow the love in your heart
and be open to all the possibilities in your life

Resplendent

If ever the Universe wanted a person to shout about it's you! You are a glittering light in this world.

Whatever your own views about yourself are, right now you need to be told how wonderful you are. You've had an awful lot to deal with in your life so far, but through it all you've maintained a heart of gold.

You may have felt that you are the only person concerned with matters around you, but the fact is that you are a constant light. You have kept the love in your heart and cared for others, and that counts for a lot in the karma stakes.

Your present life is full of promise, if you but take the time to see it. Whatever your question was when pulling this Cut-Out, apply the concept that your current concern can be broken down and dealt with in baby steps.

That is, even if it seems to be consuming you and swallowing you up, step back and try to take a more distanced look at the situation. If you look at it clearly, then you can make the effort to break it up into stages. Take each of these stages and sort them out, one by one. You will find that if you address your concerns (whether love, finance, work or health issues) methodically and carefully, your problems will be righted.

Your strength is in your psyche. You are one of the beautiful beings. Intrinsically in the goodness, light and love that shines out from you. You have a wealth of new opportunities ahead of you, which you must go for when they become apparent.

You also have the ability to teach and it would be very fulfilling if you did. Even if it were just one person you taught your knowledge to, it would have a profound effect on your life.

You are a bright light in the constellation. Always follow the love in your heart and be open to all the possibilities in your life. Bless you!

See the Funny Side

Lighten your demeanour so
that the Heavens may help you

See the Funny Side

The situation you find yourself in will be easier to deal with if you can but see the funny side of it.

No matter how grave your situation, you are being asked to lighten your demeanour. The worse you feel about things, the heavier your aura becomes.

Even if you are praying for help, your heaviness of heart is making it really difficult for your Guardian Angel to be able to help you.

The more you focus on the things in your situation that are negative, the more of the same you will attract.

If you have lost a loved one, the more miserable you are, the more you tie them to this Earth plain. They are unable to progress in the way that they should, because they are very concerned with you but cannot help you, as you are blocking any help that the Heavens want to give you.

Focus on all the good in that person. Know that they are there and send them love. Pray directly to Jesus for Higher Love and the support that you need to assist you in accepting and living through this situation.

If your problem is of a different nature but, nevertheless, overwhelming you, try to distance yourself long enough to lighten your manner. Wear bright colours and stay away from black clothes for as long as you can. Drink plenty of water and try to avoid alcohol as it may make you feel good at the time, but too much can cause depression the following day. Taking Bach Flower Rescue Remedies may help as well.

Also consider wearing or holding crystals. Amethyst balances out highs and lows, promoting emotional centering. Also helpful is Rose Quartz as it encourages self-forgiveness and acceptance, invoking self-trust and self-worth.

Remember, lightening your spirit will open you up to a better way of dealing with your situation.

Self-Esteem

Time to love yourself and put yourself first in order to accomplish your full potential

Self-Esteem

You have been neglectful and now it is beginning to show. The indications are that you have everything going for you but, because of your disregard of yourself, you are certainly not fulfilling your potential.

You may have been over-stretched by others monopolizing your time. Or it may just be that you have been focussing your attentions on the wrong things for you. Either way you need to face up to your overall situation and health, and to start to look after yourself properly. Your life is so full of promise, yet you have been ignoring the possibilities that are there for you, either deliberately or unintentionally.

You have always put other people or pursuits first in your life, often to your own detriment, and the Universe is drawing to your attention that it is time to take a look at yourself. To truly accomplish your full potential in life, firstly you need to look after and fully love yourself.

If your concerns need a straight answer then the indications are that if you accept and apply yourself to the matter in hand, it will be demanding but, as long as you don't forget about looking after yourself, you will benefit from the experience. If you say 'no' to your concern, then it will take time to come to terms with matters but, as long as you make the effort to avoid despondency and lift yourself mentally out of any sorrow, you will be able to advance back on track in a more positive fashion.

Whenever you have the option choose to spend time outdoors, as being in the open air will help to energise you. Meditation will also help, as well as making sure that you steer clear of any negative situations, people or thinking. Make a list of all the good things about you and your life as it is now, and when you feel downcast check your list and give thanks to the Universe for all the good in your life.

Slow and Steady

Your future holds rewards in store for you
far greater than you can imagine

Slow and Steady

You have to be firm and centered. This gives you a secure basis from which you can grow.

It seems that you are near the beginning of a new venture. It could be that this is a business you have started or one that you are thinking about. Be assured that you are on the right track. By taking things steadily and carefully you will build up from a firm basis. You need to keep calm and steady. No rush decisions or extravagant excesses. Keep things simple. Do things that you can afford and organize well.

Slow and steady is the order of the day. By following this principle your future holds rewards in store for you, far greater than you can imagine.

If your concerns are financial, then by staying calm you will come out on top. If your concerns are around the heart, then know that ultimately you are destined to be with your soul mate.

Whatever it is that concerns you about your present situation, think about taking things slowly and not being too hasty.

You have a lot of favourable qualities about you, which are waiting to be used. You are not limited in your gifts and, as time goes by, you will discover more areas that you can expand into. If feeling unsure or unhappy, take time to indulge yourself in pleasurable pursuits. Light a scented candle - have a deep, relaxing perfumed bath or aromatic steam sauna - drink hot chocolate or toast marshmallows in comfort; whatever it is that touches all your senses, indulge yourself. You deserve it.

Onwards and upwards! Good things come in small packages.

With the knowledge that you can trust your inner feelings, and that your future is well aspected, allow yourself to move forward in life with confidence. The best is yet to come!

Spirituality

You are encouraged to accept and develop
your Divine gifts further

Spirituality

Everyone is born with the ability to tap into his or her own spirituality. Whether you do or not is your own personal choice. This Cut-Out indicates that you are spiritually gifted and that you are in a position to develop and expand your gifts further.

If you already give readings there are indications that you are not acknowledging just how powerful your gifts are. Take time to meditate and connect with your Spirit Guides. Ask for the Christ White Light of Protection. Draw the dark colour purple into your consciousness from your third eye; luxuriate in the colour - feeling it covering you - and thank the Universe for your spiritual gifts. Finish by visualizing bright white light emanating from within you to as far as you can send it out with love. Always make sure that you are properly grounded when you work and ask your Doorkeeper to protect you. Do not doubt yourself; understand and accept that you are more than qualified to do this work.

Even if you are a spiritual beginner, you are encouraged to open up to your capabilities. Notice your feelings. Keep a notebook and acknowledge déjà vu and synchronistic events. The more you recognize and accept these signs, will increase their frequency. Don't be frightened. If you receive 'impressions' but feel frightened repeat, "Please go away if you don't walk with Christ" three times and you are safe.

Feel secure as the Universe is encouraging you to develop your spirituality. Your spirit guides are there to help you if you but ask them to.

On a more basic level, opening yourself up to communication with your Guardian Angel and requesting their help on any matter, from small things to larger issues, will get you more in tune with your life path and help you on your way. The spirits are not there to judge you, they are there to help you - you only have to ask!

Take Care

Be on your guard against deception
and it won't faze you at all

Take Care

There is something in your life that is not ringing true for you right now. This can be taken one of two ways.

It could be that you have not been straight with someone in some way. Maybe you were building yourself up to impress, or telling a white lie so as not to offend, but as time has gone by what was innocent at first is really not helping you now.

If this is the case then you may be finding it too hard to backtrack. However, this is a learning curve that you can benefit from. What you give out, you get back and honesty is always the best policy. Don't try to be something you are not as it will only lead to unease and discomfort. Take this as an opportunity to be proud about who you are and what you can do. You only have this one life to show others how unique you are. If you suspect that you have been taken in by someone, then understand that they are all 'hot air', which will ultimately fizzle out and come to nothing.

In love matters, someone may have shown you their best side and said all the right things, but you need to take a break from them so that you can get a sense of perspective and cool the ardour that is distorting your judgement. With distance you will be able to see the situation more clearly and decide which way you want to go with the relationship.

With work issues, there is someone who is all bluff, possibly even taking recognition for other people's ideas. The truth will come out eventually, as they cannot keep the pretence up forever. Stay strong and you will find that you will win out in the end. If self-employed or embarking on a new venture, be careful of anyone who promises more than they can deliver. Caution is the key with pulling this Cut-Out. Pre-warned is pre-armed and will help you to avoid being taken in by bogus, flattering 'yes' men who seek to deceive. This is nothing you can't deal with easily.

The Law of Attraction

Anything is possible as long as
you apply yourself fully

The Law of Attraction

The Universe is at work. Your prayers are being answered, governed by the Law of Attraction.

The Law of Attraction means just that. We create our own realities. We attract things we want and we also attract things we don't want. We attract the people in our lives, the stuff in our homes and the money in our bank accounts through our thoughts and feelings.

You are strong enough to deal with the situation that you find yourself in. The Universe does not give you anything you cannot deal with.

You will benefit more than you realise from your present situation. Your future ahead is bright. Your prayers are being answered, but not necessarily in the way that you had thought that things would happen. This Cut-Out indicates that your outcome will actually prove better than you have wished for. This is a shift forward in your existence, that will help you in completing this particular learning stage of your life.

By picking this Cut-Out, the Universe wants you to know that anything is possible for you so long as you apply yourself fully. You must make your wishes clear to the Universe when saying what you choose to have in your life. Then you need to truly believe that what you are asking for will become yours, without doubt, because the idea that failure is a possibility will obstruct you from getting what you want. Finally, it is important that you are open to receive. You need to know that you are deserving and worthy. When opportunities come your way do not hesitate, be active in taking the chances that you are given and feel thankful.

Repeat this affirmation to help you on your way, "Thank you for all the wealth and abundance in my life and for Divine direction placing me always in the right place at the perfect time. I am safe and well protected. Thank you Life!"

Think Positive

The solution is closer to you and more
rewarding than you think

Think Positive

Life is full of opportunities. You are not in a 'Yes' or 'No' situation if you consider all things carefully.

Having picked this Cut-Out indicates that it is really important that you think positively. Make a conscious effort to check your thoughts and what you say. Every time you are negative - change it to a positive.

You create the world you live in by what you think, say and do. Be careful that what you put out is what you would like to get back.

It seems that the solution to your problem may be nearer than you think. There are so many opportunities and choices around and ahead of you. Clear your mind and body of any negativity that you may be holding onto. Then allow yourself to explore all the possibilities that you can think of.

Be careful that you are not overcomplicating your matter of concern. Are you overlooking simpler options? Look for the solutions that are closer to home.

If your concern is money, maybe you can sell things or even ask for help from a relative or close friend?

If your concern is love and you are in a relationship where there is an issue, be brave and talk to your partner. Be honest and giving, and work to sort things out. If you have a lack of love, perhaps there is someone you know who would be glad to share an evening with you? Or perhaps a friend who is also single, who might join you in going out to mix with and meet new people?

Whatever your problem, the solution is closer than you think and more rewarding. The more positively you think, the more you will open up the myriad of opportunities that are there for you. Life should never be dull for you so a good affirmation to help you on your way is, " My life is harmonious and positive. I am safe and Divinely protected."

Transformation

Positive change awaits you
Have faith – you can do it!

Transformation

If you have been feeling unsure about things recently, indications are that the truth will be made clear to you.

You are being urged to lift your spirits up and have more faith in yourself. You may have fallen into self-doubt and worries, over matters that concern you, but by picking this Cut-Out you are being told to hold your head up high.

Being critical can lead to imagining things as being worse than they really are. You need to re-affirm how special and unique you are.

Look in the mirror frequently and say how much you love yourself. Be grateful for all that you are and all that you have. The future holds so many more areas for you to succeed and grow into.

Watch out for synchronistic events and any feelings of déjà vu as this will reaffirm that you are in the right place at the perfect time.

There is no such thing as coincidence and as long as you are feeling stronger in yourself, your Guardian Angel will be able to guide you in the right direction if you ask.

Things will become clearer to you and you will be able to see what you need to do. Be confident and truthful in all your actions, as what you give out is what you will receive.

You are so close to transformations in your life. Being more positive about yourself and your abilities will make you more open to positive change.

The Universe supports you and will open doors for you, but you have to open yourself up first. Loving yourself and having faith in yourself will allow your Guardian Angel to assist you - so long as you ask. Positive change awaits you. Be brave and help your transformation to happen. Possessing clarity about what you choose to have in your life will speed up your manifestations. Have faith. You can do it!

True Love

Follow your heart and have faith that your
needs are being taken care of

True Love

This is true love of the highest nature. Whether past or present this Cut-Out is abundant with love!

The seeds have been sown and love is at the heart of your situation.

Whatever stage of your life you are at, the answer is love. If you have been defensive of yourself then the answer is that love is there for you.

It is safe to accept and let someone into your life. You won't be let down as it is time for you to feel safe in a relationship.

If you have challenges up ahead of you then follow your heart. Find solutions that come from the infinite well of love that is deep inside you. If you approach your problems from an intention of love, then that allows you to solve and heal situations with goodwill and care.

If you are feeling fearful about your situation then affirm frequently, "I am surrounded by love. I am Divinely protected and guided. All is well in my world. I am safe!"

It is important to banish any fears you have and find your inner serenity. Once you are calm you will find that you are able to approach your problems from a more secure footing. Choosing the option that utilizes love at its core will pay dividends.

People that you love need handling with sensitivity, and a little consideration and patience will go a long way.

Make an effort to do random acts of kindness on a daily basis, even as small as smiling at someone, and you will improve your well-being and karma. The more you look at the world with loving eyes: the more love you will find in your life.

All the love in the world is there for you. Follow your heart and have faith that your needs are being taken care of. Smile often and thank the Universe for surrounding you with love.

Unique

Time to be clear about what you want
and enjoy your life

Unique

You are one of a kind, yet you are not being heard clearly. There is someone who is being stubborn and not listening to you. Life should be joyous for you but in this one concern it is leaving you lacking. Whatever is troubling you needs to be faced head on, otherwise the situation could go on for a very long time.

You are finding it hard to vocalize what you should, which does not seem usual for you. Maybe you are unsure and need to focus your thoughts more, in order to work this one out. Or you could be listening too much to what others have to say and not allowing yourself to form your own opinion.

You are a true individual and, as such, the way you look at things is sometimes unpredictable and can even be called risky.

However there is a great positive vibration around your situation right now. You are being well protected by Spirit. If you weigh up the pros and cons and take the positive approach, what you concentrate on is well-starred and the more creative you can be, the better.

However, don't let past regrets hold you back. It is not beneficial for you to hark back to former events or situations, as this feeds a negativity into you that you otherwise would not have. Each time you evoke the past, make yourself aware of the moment you are in. You cannot change anything that has gone before, but you can create what you want right now.

You are incomparable and it takes a long time for others to truly understand and appreciate you. Get out there and show the world how lovely you are. Do not shrink away from mixing with people and making new friends. The world is your proverbial oyster. Make up your mind and deal with your concerns. You need to forge ahead and get on with your life in your own inimitable way.

Verification

An Angelic proclamation of the highest order
full of promise and enrichment

Verification

This is an Angelic proclamation of the very highest order that is just for you - full of promise and enrichment. The Angels are involved with singing this message to you, which tells you just how special this is. They are singing to confirm that what lies ahead is glorious and they want you to sense the warmth of joyful feeling that they are surrounding you with.

Take time to listen to music that uplifts you, as that will help you to be on a higher frequency. Sing along or even dance to your favourite songs and lift your inner being. Practice smiling frequently and find things that amuse you, so that you can laugh out loud. Wear bright colours instead of dark colours. Put on your favourite perfume. Doing these things will allow you to manifest with more definition, when you meditate or take time out to think about that which you want in your life.

There is also an exotic flavour here, which means that if you are considering anything to do with another country or race - for instance; travel, marriage, business, study, friendship or the like - know that it will enhance your life, bringing in a new dimension to it and can even change your life path for the better.

If you need an answer to a specific question, then the answer is most definitely 'Yes'. You should ask your Guardian Angel to show you what you should do now, and request them to smooth your path. Remember you are not alone and they want, and are there, to help you if you ask.

If finances are uppermost in your mind, know that money is well aspected. You may be in for a windfall of some type, either inherited or an unexpected win. Keep an eye out for nuggets of information. These will come along when you least expect them to. You need to be alert to accepting the direction that they encourage you to follow. You are Divinely blessed.

Wonderment

Spirit is sending you love and help
Look after yourself

Wonderment

Jewels of calm are being given to you. Moments of oasis are being sent to you from spirit as they want to soothe and relax you, and give you that inner shot of love that you are dry of and in need of.

Life seems complicated and way too hard. But each step is a learning curve and, although it is not what you want to hear, every tribulation that you negotiate and beat, makes you stronger.

Don't wail, "But all I want is a quiet life" because that is not what you've agreed to. Try shifting the balance around and know that each obstacle which you leave in your wake, likens you to a gladiator and shows true grit in adversity.

There is so much love coming from spirit. There is a loved one, a parent or grandparent who multiplies love to you, as only a parent can. They look out for you, and when you ask for help they are always there, guiding your way. Their love is eternal and you are very blessed to have that knowledge of spirit protection.

You may find things very difficult sometimes, but you will always pull through. You will never be unable to cope and, quite often, will come out on top and you can't ask for better than that!

Pay attention to your health and listen to what your body is telling you. There is always a reason why something happens. From the smallest bruise to complicated illnesses, there will always be a reason why it has happened.

Quite often illnesses slow you down and make you rest. If you translate it to your present situation, you may find that it stops you rushing headlong into something that, with time, you may change your opinion about.

Try writing down your blessings as they occur. Know that they are from a loving spirit who respects you and wants you to know that they are full of admiration for you. They may not have said it to you in person, but they want you to know it now. Bless them!

Your Choice

Be true to yourself and you will find
the right path to follow

Your Choice

Your situation calls on you to make some choices. There is no right or wrong decision, however what you choose is potentially liable to determine the path you take in life.

Whatever it is that you are being torn between, if you think about it carefully you will see that one way potentially seems easier than the other.

There are so many possibilities ahead for you. The smoother more sensible path for you to take is well starred. You will find it easier and each element of your life will run alongside and fit, in a logical and pragmatic way.

Your other option is much harder and demands all your time and energy. However, it does not mean that you will be struggling all the time. What it throws up is that this choice requires you to devote more time, commitment, hard work and understanding to it. Put the work in and you will reap the benefits over time.

Whichever choice you make about the circumstances that you find yourself concerned with, the most important thing is that you ultimately make your selection with your highest good and not your ego in mind.

The easier option may also be attractive to you because you may be drawn to it by long-held beliefs from your childhood. Are these beliefs relevant to the way you are now? Is it really what you want deep down inside?

Weigh up your options. The important factor is to be true to yourself.

You only have this one shot at life. Every moment is important. You can't press rewind and start again. What you say, think and do has an immediate effect on the circumstances that you find yourself in. Be true to yourself and have faith that if you follow your heart to your Highest Good, you will be triumphant in making the right choice.

The Flower Oracle Affirmations

Good Fortune:-
I accept and delight in all the good and abundance that is flowing into my life. I am very grateful.

Junk old karma:-
I release all past negative patterns, fear and doubt. I am strong, clear and open. I receive abundance, love, light and knowledge. Thank you life.

Liberation:-
The past is finished and gone. I control my life. I choose to think clearly and positively. I live in the now.

Nurture Yourself:-
I am safe and secure. Well protected and guided.
I look after myself and my life is smooth and abundant.

Protection:-
I deserve my abundant life and I am very grateful that I manifest money easily.

The Law of Attraction:-
Thank you for all the wealth and abundance in my life, and for Divine direction placing me always in the right place at the perfect time. I am safe and well protected. Thank you life!

Think Positive:-
My life is harmonious and positive. I am safe and Divinely protected.

True Love:-
I am surrounded by love. I am Divinely protected and guided. All is well in my world. I am safe!

'The Flower Oracle' Cut-Outs

Anticipate Miracles	Apple-pie Order	Blessings
Bounty	Celebration	Commitment
Cornucopia	Dependency	Duplicity
Embarkation	Fairy Enchantment	Fragility
Good Fortune	Have Faith	Hurrah
Indecision	Intemperance	Junk old karma
Liberation	Longevity	Magnetism
New Opportunities	Nurture Yourself	Oodles of Plenty
Out with the Old, In with the New	Patience	Peregrination
Perseverance	Protection	Quicksilver
Resplendent	See the Funny Side	Self-Esteem
Slow and Steady	Spirituality	Take Care
The Law of Attraction	Think Positive	Transformation
True Love	Unique	Verification
Wonderment	Your Choice	

Visit **www.thefloweroracle.com** to download Cut-Outs

Anticipate Miracles	Apple-pie Order
Blessings	Bounty
Celebration	Commitment
Cornucopia	Dependency
Duplicity	Embarkation
Fairy Enchantment	Fragility
Good Fortune	Have Faith
Hurrah	Indecision
Intemperance	Junk old karma
Liberation	Longevity
Magnetism	New Opportunities

Visit **www.thefloweroracle.com** to download Cut-Outs

Nurture Yourself	Oodles of Plenty
Out with the Old, In with the New	Patience
Peregrination	Perseverance
Resplendent	Quicksilver
Protection	See the Funny Side
Self-Esteem	Slow and Steady
Spirituality	Take Care
The Law of Attraction	Think Positive
Transformation	True Love
Unique	Verification
Wonderment	Your Choice

Visit **www.thefloweroracle.com** to download Cut-Outs

www.ingramcontent.com/pod-product-compliance
Lightning Source LLC
Chambersburg PA
CBHW041802160426
43191CB00001B/9